OLYMPIC SPORTS

BALL SPORTS

Clive Gifford

W
FRANKLIN WATTS

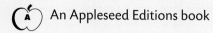 An Appleseed Editions book

Paperback edition 2012

First published in 2011 by Franklin Watts
338 Euston Road, London NW1 3BH

Franklin Watts Australia
Hachette Children's Books
Level 17/207 Kent St, Sydney, NSW 2000

© 2011 Appleseed Editions

Created by Appleseed Editions Ltd,
Well House, Friars Hill, Guestling,
East Sussex TN35 4ET

Designed by Helen James
Edited by Mary-Jane Wilkins
Picture research by Su Alexander

ISBN 978-1-4451-1392-0

Dewey Classification: 796.3

A CIP catalogue for this book is available from the British Library.

Picture credits
Page 4 Sports Illustrated/Getty Images; 5t Sunxuejun/Shutterstock, b AFP/Getty
Images; 6 AFP/Getty Images; 7 Sports Illustrated/Getty Images; 8 Bongarts/Getty
Images for DFB; 9 The FA via Getty Images; 10 & 11 Getty Images; 12 & 13 NBAE/
Getty Images; 14 Bloomberg via Getty Images; 15 & 16 AFP/Getty Images; 17 Olga
Besnard/Shutterstock; 18 Getty Images; 19,20,21,22,23 & 24 AFP/Getty Images;
25 Muzsy/Shutterstock; 26 Getty Images; 27 AFP/Getty Images; 28 Lev Radin/
Shutterstock; 29t Getty Images, b Brandon Parry/Shutterstock
Front cover: Getty Images

Printed in Singapore

Franklin Watts is a division of Hachette Children¹s Books,
an Hachette UK company.
www.hachette.co.uk

Contents

Going for gold

The Olympics is the greatest sporting show on Earth. More than 10,000 athletes (or Olympians) flock to one country, where they live in an Olympic village and compete against each other during 17 days of unforgettable action. The top performers win an Olympic gold, silver or bronze medal for finishing in the top three of their event.

The women's beach volleyball medal winners wave to the crowd at the 2008 Olympics. In the centre are gold medallists, Kerri Walsh and Misty May-Treanor from the USA.

MODERN GAMES

The modern Olympic Games began in 1896 in Athens. They revived the sporting contests held by the ancient Greeks at Olympia from 776 BCE.

Today, the Olympics are held in summer every four years. The host city and nation welcome thousands of spectators, while hundreds of millions more watch on television.

BALL SPORTS BOOM

The 1896 Olympics included just one ball sport – men's tennis. The winner, John Pius Boland, was in Greece on holiday and only decided to take part in the tennis at the last minute. Today, more than a thousand sportsmen and women take part in every Olympics, competing in a range of ball sports, both individually and in teams.

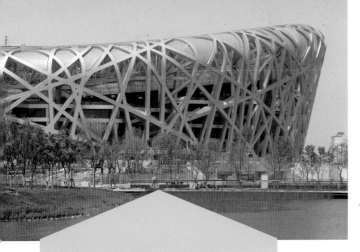

The Beijing National Stadium was used for the 2008 Olympics opening ceremony, athletics events and the football finals.

Super Star

China's table tennis legend Zhang Yining triumphed in the women's singles at the 2004 and 2008 Olympics and the team events, winning the maximum possible four gold medals. Zhang was ranked number one in the world from 2003 to 2010.

IN OR OUT?

Some ball sports which were once part of the Olympics are no longer played at the games. They include cricket, lacrosse, croquet and polo on horseback. Baseball and softball were played until 2008 but will not be part of the 2012 or 2016 games. Two ball sports rejoin the Olympics in 2016 – golf for top **professionals** and a form of rugby union called rugby sevens. This is a seven-a-side version of the sport. The teams play on the full-sized rugby pitch which is usually used by 15-player sides.

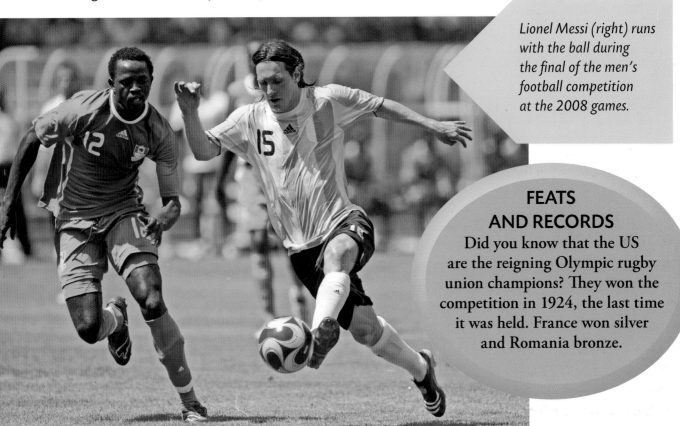

Lionel Messi (right) runs with the ball during the final of the men's football competition at the 2008 games.

FEATS AND RECORDS
Did you know that the US are the reigning Olympic rugby union champions? They won the competition in 1924, the last time it was held. France won silver and Romania bronze.

Football

The world's most popular team sport has been played at the Olympics since 1900 by men and 1996 by women. At the 2008 Olympics, a record 2,137,462 spectators watched the two tournaments.

Italy's Giuseppe Rossi takes a penalty against Belgium in the quarter finals of the 2008 Olympics. Rossi scored two penalties in this game, but his side lost 3-2.

AIM OF THE GAME

A football match lasts 90 minutes, with a 15 minute break at half time. Teams attack by moving the ball around the pitch using any part of their bodies except their arms and hands. The goalkeepers are allowed to handle the ball, but only inside their penalty area – the box surrounding their goal. The attacking team scores by shooting or heading the ball into their opponents' goal. The defending team aims to stop goals being scored against them and to gain control of the ball.

A coach or manager decides the team's **formation**. This is the way the team lines up in rows of **defenders**, **midfielders** and **attackers**.

Christie Rampone (right) about to tackle Brazil's Renata Costa during the 2008 Olympic final. Rampone was captain of the USA team which won the match 1-0 and the gold medal.

goal

penalty area

penalty spot

centre circle

Football pitches vary in length between 90 and 120 metres. Pitches are split into two halves and each end has a 40.3m wide penalty area around the goal.

eight teams entering the **knockout** rounds (quarter finals, semi-finals and the final). In the knockout stages, a drawn game goes into extra time and if the scores are still level, there is a **penalty** shoot-out. Each team takes five penalties and if neither team is ahead, there is a sudden death shoot-out. Only one Olympic final has been decided this way, when Cameroon beat Spain 5-3 on penalties in 2000.

Tactics can change during a game and the coach can swap up to three of his players with **substitutes** to freshen up their play.

IT'S A KNOCKOUT

Sixteen teams take part in the men's Olympics football tournament and 12 in the women's. They are placed in groups of four with the top

Olympic OoPs

A combined Great Britain side competed in the Olympics until 1972. In 1952 they suffered an embarrassing defeat against Luxembourg 5-3. Their worst ever Olympic defeat was in the 1956 games when they lost 6-1 to Bulgaria.

German striker Birgit Prinz (centre) powers forward between two Danish defenders. Prinz holds the record for the most goals scored in a single Olympics match (four against China in 2004). She shares this record with Brazil's Cristiane.

FEATS AND RECORDS
The US women's team have lost just two of 24 matches at four Olympics. They won gold medals in1996, 2004 and 2008 and silver in 2000.

EARLY CHAMPIONS
During the 1920s a strong team from Uruguay won the 1924 and 1928 Olympics and then the first **World Cup** in 1930. After the Second World War, eastern European nations won every tournament from 1952 to 1988, except in 1984, when France won.

PROS ALLOWED
Only **amateur** football players were allowed to compete in the games until 1984. Today, all the 18 players in a squad can be professional, but at least 15 must be under 23 years old. Ronaldinho, for example, was 28 years old when he played

for Brazil at the 2008 Olympics and won a bronze medal. There are no age restrictions in the women's tournament, so top female stars such as Brazil's Marta and US legend Mia Hamm can play.

The 2012 Olympic football final will be played at the new Wembley Stadium. Other matches will be played at Manchester United's Old Trafford stadium, the Millennium Stadium in Cardiff, Hampden Park, Glasgow and St James' Park, Newcastle.

SHOCK RESULTS

Football matches can be low-scoring and can have unexpected results. At the 2004 Olympics, Iraq knocked out a Portuguese team which included Cristiano Ronaldo and **outsiders** Paraguay beat Italy 1-0 , reaching the final of the men's tournament.

Basketball

Basketball is played with five players a side. It was invented by Canadian gym instructor James Naismith in 1891 and first appeared at the Olympics in 1936. At the Olympics, 12 men's and 12 women's teams contest matches which last 40 minutes, split into four ten-minute quarters.

COURT SPORT

At the Olympics, basketball games are played on a 28m long court, split into two, with a high hoop at each end. Players score baskets by shooting the ball through the hoop from above. Shots made from within a D-shaped arc, called the three point line, at each end of the court score two points. Shots from outside the arc score three points.

Players move the basketball around the court by **passing** it to teammates, or **dribble** by bouncing the ball with one hand as they move. Once they start dribbling, players cannot stop, hold the ball and start to dribble again. If they do the ball goes to their opponents. Players use a range of chest, bounce and overhead passes over different distances. They also make fake moves or passes, to trick opponents.

COUNTING DOWN

Basketball games are quick, sharp and ferocious. Teams have just 24 seconds from when they receive the ball to make a shot, otherwise the ball goes to the other team. The time is displayed on a clock and as the seconds count down the tension rises. The defending team tries to **intercept** weak passes to gain the ball and each defender may **mark** an area or an opponent to stop them getting the ball.

Olympic OoPs

At the 1936 Olympics, the men's basketball final was held outdoors. Rain turned the dirt court into a sea of mud so the players could not dribble the ball. Joe Fortenberry was the highest scorer with just seven points as the US beat Canada 19-8. Major competitions are now held indoors!

FEATS AND RECORDS

The women's US and Australian teams have contested the final of the last three Olympics, with the Australians having to settle for silver every time.

Lauren Jackson of Australia dribbles the ball as she drives forward past a Chinese defender. Australia won this 2008 semi-final match, but lost 92-65 in the final.

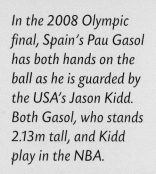

In the 2008 Olympic final, Spain's Pau Gasol has both hands on the ball as he is guarded by the USA's Jason Kidd. Both Gasol, who stands 2.13m tall, and Kidd play in the NBA.

FEATS AND RECORDS

Lithuania is one of the smallest countries ever to reach the Olympic basketball tournament – fewer than 3.5 million people live there. Their Olympic teams have won three bronze medals and come fourth twice in the last five Olympics.

REBOUNDS

When a shot misses and the ball cannons off the hoop or the backboard behind, both teams compete for the ball. This is called rebounding. A team that wins most rebounds usually wins the game. At the 2008 Olympics, Iran's Hamed Haddadi grabbed an average of more than 11 rebounds every game.

GIANTS OF THE GAME

Top basketball players are tall, often over 1.95m in height. The tallest woman to win an Olympic gold medal in any sport was Soviet basketball player Iuliana Semenova. She stood 2.18m tall and won gold in both 1976 and 1980. In the men's game, China's Yao Ming is one of the tallest players ever – a towering 2.29m tall.

BASKETBALL LEAGUES

Away from the Olympics, the world's leading professional league is the National Basketball

Association (NBA) in North America. Many foreign stars play for NBA teams, including Spain's Pau Gasol, Argentina's Manu Ginobili and Britain's Luol Deng, who plays for the Chicago Bulls. A similar league for female players, the WNBA, began in 1997. Lauren Jackson, captain of the Australian team and an Olympic silver medallist, plays in the WNBA.

DREAM TEAMS

Professional basketball players were first allowed to compete in the 1992 Olympics, held in Barcelona. The US 'dream team' included top NBA stars including Michael Jordan, Magic Johnson and Larry Bird. They won the tournament easily. Since then, US teams have included talented players such as Shaquille O'Neal, Kevin Garnett and Kobe Bryant. They have won gold medals at every games, except the 2004 Olympics. There, Lithuania, Puerto Rico and Argentina all defeated the US team, and Argentina took the gold medal.

Olympic OoPs

The US team boycotted the medals ceremony at the 1972 Olympics after a final match where they believed that the Soviet Union's winning score came after the game was over. The US team's silver medals remain uncollected.

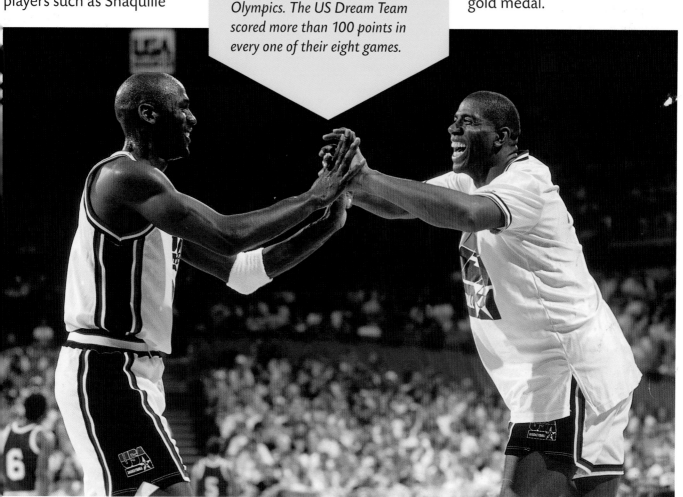

Basketball legends Michael Jordan (left) and Magic Johnson celebrate during the 1992 Barcelona Olympics. The US Dream Team scored more than 100 points in every one of their eight games.

Tennis

Tennis players competed at the Olympics from 1896 to 1924. After a gap of 64 years, tennis was played again at the 1988 Olympics in Seoul. Miloslav Mecir and Steffi Graf won gold medals in the singles.

Swiss tennis players Roger Federer (right) with partner Stanislas Wawrinka face Americans Bob and Mike Bryan in their 2008 Olympic semi-final match. Federer and Wawrinka won the match 7-6, 6-4.

SERVE AND RETURN

Tennis players compete on a rectangular court which is 23.8m long and divided in two by a net. They hit the ball over the net with stringed rackets. Each point starts with one player making a **serve**, a powerful overhead shot from behind the back of the court, into their opponent's service court. Some powerful servers, such as Andy Roddick, can strike the ball at speeds of over 230 km/h!

RALLIES

Once the ball is in play, a **rally** begins. Each player strikes the ball, trying to hit a winning shot that their opponent cannot reach. Top players need to be fit and **agile** so they can change direction quickly and chase down the ball. Some rallies are over in a short, sharp series of two or three shots. Others last for 15 or more shots. Matches in the Olympics can last for three hours or longer, so players also need great **stamina**.

Super Star

Roger Federer is considered to be one of the best male tennis players of all time. He has won 16 **grand slam** singles titles, but never the Olympic singles competition. He met his wife, tennis player Mirka Vavrinec, at the 2000 Olympics and in 2008 won the doubles with fellow Swiss tennis player, Stanislas Wawrinka.

SINGLES AND DOUBLES

A total of 64 men and 64 women take part in Olympic singles tournaments. These are the top players in the world rankings. A handful of players, such as those returning after an injury, are given a **wild card** which allows them to compete. Thirty-two pairs of men and women contest the doubles. In 2012 there will be a mixed doubles competition too.

doubles sideline

singles sideline

baseline

service line

net

centre service line

A tennis court has two sets of sidelines. The wider lines are used in doubles matches and the narrower ones in singles matches.

FEATS AND RECORDS

Only one tennis player has won both the singles and doubles at the same Olympic Games since 1988 – Chile's Nicolás Massú in 2004.

Dinara Safina completes a serve. Safina beat the world number one Jelena Janković and won a silver medal in the 2008 Olympics singles.

Elena Dementieva shows her delight as she wins an Olympic gold medal in 2008. She beat Dinara Safina in the final: 3-6, 7-5, 6-3. Dementieva also won a silver medal at the 2000 Olympics.

FEATS AND RECORDS

Elena Dementieva won the women's singles at the 2008 games, and fellow Russians Dinara Safina and Vera Zvonareva took silver and bronze. This was the first time one country had won all three singles medals since 1908.

SCORING SYSTEM

Tennis has an unusual scoring system. A match is broken down into sets of games. At the Olympics, a player has to win two sets to beat an opponent. Players who reach the finals of the men's singles and doubles have to win three sets to take the match. To win a set, players have to win six games and be at least two games ahead of their opponent, so 6-4 and 7-5 are set-winning scores. If the players win six games each, they play a **tiebreaker** to decide who takes the set. When they reach 6-6 in the fifth set of a final or the third set of other matches, players have to continue until one wins two more games than their opponent.

ON TOUR

Away from the Olympics, the top tennis players take part in men's (ATP) and women's (WTA) professional tours and play tournaments almost every week from January to November. Dotted throughout the year are four tournaments rated more highly than the rest – the Australian Open, French Open, Wimbledon and the US Open. These four are grand slam tournaments and they are the tournaments that tennis players most want to win.

HUGE IMPORTANCE

Only 11 of the world's top 20 men competed at the 1988 Olympics, and only three of the top ten men competed in 1996. Today, players who compete at an Olympics win points which count towards their position on the professional tour. The 2008 singles competitions included 17 of the top 20 men, and 18 of the top 20 women.

FEATS AND RECORDS

Lleyton Hewitt and Chris Guccione played 57 games to beat Agustin Calleri and Juan Monaco at the 2008 Olympics men's doubles (4-6, 7-6, 18-16). This was the highest number of games ever played in a three set match at an Olympics.

BRONZE PLAY-OFF

In 1988 and 1992, the two losers at the semi-final stage both received a bronze medal. Since then, the two have to play a further match to decide who wins the bronze. In 2000, Frenchman Arnaud Di Pasquale beat Roger Federer to win the bronze.

Rafael Nadal of Spain hits a powerful forehand. In 2008, Nadal beat Lleyton Hewitt, Novak Djokovic and Fernando Gonzalez on the way to winning Olympic gold.

Super Star

US star Andre Agassi was in fine form during the 1996 Olympics men's singles. Most finals last three or four hours, but Andre won his final against Spain's Sergi Bruguera in just 77 minutes.

Table tennis

Table tennis has been an Olympic sport since 1988. In many parts of Asia table tennis stars become celebrities in the same way as footballers in Europe or basketball players in the United States.

Wang Hao of China serves in the final of the table tennis at the 2008 games. Wang and partner Wang Liqin beat the German pair, Christian Suess and Timo Boll to win the gold medal.

TABLE TOP GAME

Players compete on a table measuring 2.74m by 1.525m divided by a net. They hit the ball across the table, making sure that the first bounce is on their opponent's side. They score a point if the ball bounces more than once on their opponent's side of the table or if one player cannot keep the ball in play.

WINNING GAMES

A game is won when a player has scored 11 points and is two points ahead of an opponent. If the score is 10-10, the game continues until they reach a score such as 12-10 or 13-11. In singles matches at the Olympics, the first player to win four games wins the match and knocks out their opponent.

BAT AND BALL

A table tennis ball is hollow and light, weighing just 2.7 grams. Players use small rackets (also called bats or paddles) covered in rubber. Skilled players spin the ball to make it loop and swerve in the air so that it changes direction when it lands on the table. Top players also hit powerful smash shots, sending the ball flying at speeds of over 100 km/h.

FEATS AND RECORDS

At the 2008 Olympics, Singapore won its first medal since 1960. Li Jiawei, Feng Tianwei and Wang Yuegu won silver in the women's team table tennis competition.

FEATS AND RECORDS

China has an amazing record at Olympic table tennis. Chinese table tennis players have won 20 of the 24 gold medals contested since 1988, as well as 13 silvers and eight bronzes!

TEAM TABLE TENNIS

Since the 2008 Olympics doubles table tennis has been a team competition. A country's team plays four singles and one doubles match. The first team to win three matches goes on to the next round.

China's Guo Yue hits a delicate shot against Singapore's Jiawei in the match for the women's singles bronze medal. Top players like Yue put huge amounts of spin on the ball.

Field hockey

Field hockey is an all-action, 11-a-side team sport. Players use a wooden stick to push, flick and power a small, solid ball around a large pitch. The aim of the game is to score goals by shooting the ball past the other team's goalkeeper and into the goal.

Japan's Kaori Chiba dribbles the ball past German defenders at the 2008 Olympics. A hockey match lasts 70 minutes, split into two 35-minute halves.

Olympic oops

India scored a marvellous victory at the 1932 Olympic games. In front of the US team's home crowd in Los Angeles, Roop Singh scored ten goals as they won 24-1. The American team next lost to Japan 9-1.

HOCKEY HISTORY

Hockey began in the 19th century and has been played by men at the Olympics since 1908 and by women since 1980. The Olympics joins the World Cup (held since 1971 for men and 1974 for women) as the leading competition for the sport.

SQUAD AND SCORING

A hockey squad has 16 players – 11 on the pitch and five substitutes. Players can be subbed on and off the pitch any number of times. The goalkeeper wears lots of protection and is allowed to handle the ball, which can travel at more than 100 km/h. If another player touches the ball the umpire gives the ball to the other team.

Players score goals from inside a large semi-circle in front of each goal. At major tournaments a video umpire helps the on-field umpires by watching replays to check whether or not a goal has been scored.

Dutch goalkeeper Lisanne de Roever uses her stick to stop a shot during a match against China. A goalkeeper can use any part of her body to stop a shot.

FEATS AND RECORDS

The German Keller family started their marvellous medal haul in 1936 when Erwin Keller won a silver. His son Carsten won a gold in 1972 and his grandsons Andreas (in 1992), Florian (2008) and granddaughter Natascha (2004) all won gold medals playing hockey. Outstanding!

Spain's Victor Sojo controls the ball while German defender Timo Wess moves to tackle him. This was the 2008 men's Olympic final, when Germany beat Spain 1-0.

GAME PLAY

Hockey players need to be fit, fast and strong. A player uses the flat face of the wooden hockey stick to pass the ball to teammates or dribble it past opponents in a series of taps and nudges. Defenders watch and wait before tackling with the blade of their stick or poking the ball out of an opponent's control.

SIMPLY THE BEST

Only the best teams play at the Olympics. Twelve women's and 12 men's teams qualify in tournaments beforehand, such as the Asian Games or the Euro Hockey competition. Teams are divided into two groups and play each team in their group. The top two from each group contest semi-finals, then the winners play for the gold medal and the losing sides play for bronze.

A hockey pitch is 55m wide and 91.4m long. In the past, pitches at top tournaments were grass but they are now made from artificial turf, which runs fast and true.

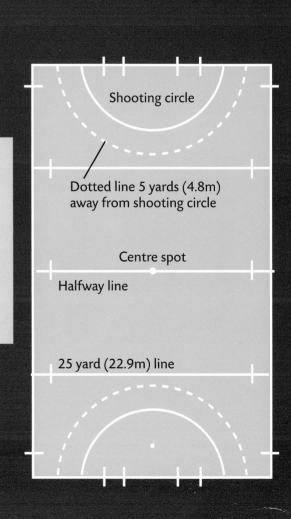

Shooting circle

Dotted line 5 yards (4.8m) away from shooting circle

Centre spot

Halfway line

25 yard (22.9m) line

TIGHT AND TENSE

Many hockey matches are close and may be decided by a single goal. In the semi-final and final of the Olympics, a game which ends in a draw goes into 15 minutes of extra time. If the scores are still level after this, there is a penalty shoot-out, similar to the one in soccer. Each shot is taken from a penalty spot, 6.2m from the goal.

Super Star

Dutch defender Minke Booij is one of the greatest female hockey players in the world. In 2000, she won a bronze medal, a silver in 2004 and, finally, gold in 2008.

FEATS AND RECORDS

The Zimbabwe women's hockey team had a last-minute invitation to the 1980 Olympics when another country dropped out. They had just ten days to prepare but eventually won Zimbabwe's first Olympic gold medal in any sport.

MEDAL MASTERS

Between 1928 and 1968, India and Pakistan won every Olympics with India the all-time leading gold medallists with eight. In recent times, Germany, Australia and the Netherlands have been the most successful sides.

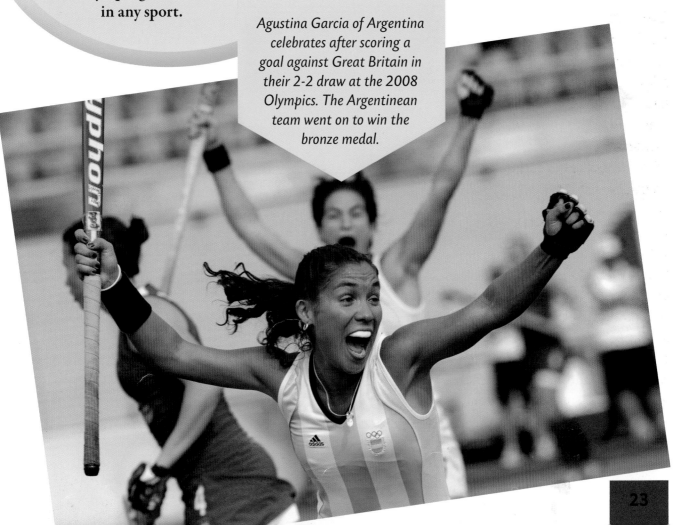

Agustina Garcia of Argentina celebrates after scoring a goal against Great Britain in their 2-2 draw at the 2008 Olympics. The Argentinean team went on to win the bronze medal.

Volleyball

Volleyball was invented in 1895 by William G. Morgan as a less energetic version of basketball. Modern volleyball is very fast and players need to be agile and have lightning fast reactions.

A point begins with a leaping serve made by a player from beyond the back of the court into their opponent's court. A player continues serving until their team loses a point.

AIM OF THE GAME

An indoor volleyball court is 18m long and divided into two by a net which is over two metres high. Players keep a ball in the air using their hands, arms or body. A team is allowed to touch the ball three times (with no player touching it twice in a row), before the ball must cross the net into the other team's court. Matches are played in sets, with 25 points needed to win a set, but only 15 points needed to win the final fifth set.

SERVE AND DEFEND

Each point begins with a serve by a player standing beyond the back of the court. This player continues to serve until his team loses a point. Defending teams try to stop the ball hitting the floor, diving to keep the ball in the air or leaping to block it with their arms at the net.

OLYMPIC VOLLEYBALL

Volleyball was demonstrated at the 1924 Olympics but it did not become part of the games until 40 years later. At the 2000 Olympics the rules were changed so that every team now has a specialist defender called a libero, who doesn't serve and wears a different coloured top. Today either team can score, regardless of who serves.

A Hungarian volleyball player spikes the ball by hitting it powerfully over the net with an overarm motion. The opposing player leaps and raises both arms to try to block the shot.

Super Star

Inna Ryskal has won more volleyball medals than anyone else. She won silver in 1964 and 1976 and gold in 1968 and 1972 as part of the Soviet Union team.

Olympic OoPs

At the 1988 Olympics, Peru's women's team were two sets up and just one point away from beating the Soviet Union, but they eventually lost the match by three sets to two.

Beach volleyball

Beach volleyball was first played at the Olympics in 1996. It is an exciting version of volleyball with just two players per side. Both the men's and women's tournaments include 24 pairs and every country can send two teams.

This men's 2008 beach volleyball semi-final was between two Brazilian teams. Ricardo Santos (right) has been at three Olympics, winning a silver medal in 2000, gold in 2004 and bronze in 2008.

RULES OF THE GAME

Beach volleyball has similar rules to volleyball. A team can touch the ball three times before sending it over the net. The beach volleyball ball is slightly larger and softer and the court is covered with sand. Only two players compete and no substitutions are allowed, so the game is a test of fitness and stamina as well as skill.

Top players are very agile and can dive sharply to retrieve a ball as well as leaping high to block an opponent's shot at the net. Top pairs from

Super Star

Misty May-Treanor and Kerri Walsh are the only beach volleyball pair to win Olympic gold medals at two games in a row. When they beat China's Tian Jia and Wang Jie to win their second gold medal in 2008, it was their 108th win in a row.

A team wins a set by reaching 21 points and if the scores are level after two sets, a third tiebreaker set is played to 15 points. Teams change ends on the court every seven points or after every five points in the tiebreaker set.

Bringing in the beach

The beach volleyball competition at the 2012 Olympics will be held in Horse Guards Parade in the centre of London. Many tonnes of sand will be imported into London for the arena which will hold up to 15,000 spectators.

countries such as the US, Italy, China and Brazil work closely together and one player often sets up their teammate for a powerful overarm shot over the net called a spike. Players signal their next move to a teammate with a hand behind their back where their opponents can't see it.

FEATS AND RECORDS
Stefan Kobel and Patrick Heuscher won a bronze medal in beach volleyball at the 2004 Olympics. Not bad, considering they come from Switzerland, a mountainous country with no coast or beaches.

American Elaine Youngs dives at full stretch to try to reach the ball before it hits the sand. If the ball lands in her court, her team loses the point.

Gold medal greats

Many competitors train hard and make sacrifices to perform at their best at an Olympics. Competition is fierce in all ball sports, so only the most talented take part. Here are the stories of four great Olympic sportspeople.

VENUS WILLIAMS

Venus Williams has been the most successful competitor at tennis since the sport rejoined the Olympics in 1988. She has won three gold medals (two in 2000 and one in 2008). She has also won five Wimbledon singles tournaments and two other singles grand slam events. In the women's doubles she plays with her sister, Serena, and has won a further 11 grand slam women's doubles titles, including the 2010 Australian Open.

FEATS AND RECORDS
Venus Williams recorded the fastest serve by a woman at a grand slam tournament when she hit a serve measured at a blistering 206 km/h at the 2007 French Open.

Venus Williams prepares to play one of her trademark powerful shots.

CHARLES KIRALY

Charles learned to play volleyball from his father, a Hungarian doctor, on the beaches of California, USA. He was a member of the US volleyball team that won at the 1984 Olympics and was captain when they repeated the feat in 1988.

Charles was an athletic player with a powerful shot, who also won at World Championships. He switched to beach volleyball and with his partner Kent Steffes won the first Olympic beach volleyball tournament in 1996.

TEUN DE NOOIJER

Dutch field hockey player Teun de Nooijer played at his first Olympics in 1996. His skill helped to win the Netherlands their first ever Olympic gold medal. The team won the 2000 Olympics, gained a silver at the 2004 games and finished fourth in 2008. In 2009, Teun played his 400th game for his country, winning a 5-3 victory over India.

Teun de Nooijer wheels away after scoring another goal for the Netherlands.

LISA LESLIE

Women's basketball star Lisa Leslie competed at four Olympics in a row from 1996, winning a gold medal every time. In 2004, Leslie became the all-time leading point scorer of the US women's team as well as its most successful rebounder at the Olympics. Leslie captained the team at her last Olympics in 2008. She was also the first woman to perform a slam dunk – scoring by leaping above the basket and pushing the ball down through the hoop – in the WNBA professional basketball league.

Lisa Leslie pauses to shoot. The star basketballer scored 6,263 points during her WNBA career.

Glossary

agile   If you are agile you can move your body, or parts of it, very quickly while keeping them under control.

amateur   Someone who plays a sport without being paid to do so.

attacker   In many ball sports, attackers are players whose main aim is to score goals or points, or to create chances for their team to score.

defender   In many ball sports, defenders are players whose main aim is to stop goals being scored against their team.

dribble   Basketball players dribble by bouncing the ball with one hand while moving their feet. Dribbling in football and hockey means moving the ball along the ground with small taps of the feet in football and the stick in hockey.

formation   The way that a team in many ball sports line up to play.

grand slam   The name given to the four biggest tennis tournaments – the Australian Open, the French Open, Wimbledon and the US Open.

intercept   To take possession of the ball as it passes between opponents.

knockout   A way of organizing a competition so a losing player or team leaves the competition and the winner progresses.

mark   To guard an area of a court or pitch, or a player from the opposing team to prevent them scoring.

midfielder   Midfield football and hockey players are skilled in both attack and defence and play in the middle of the pitch.

outsider   A slang term to describe a player or team not likely to win a competition.

pass   To send the ball to a teammate.

penalty   A chance to score a goal in hockey and football with only the goalkeeper opposing you.

professional   A player who is paid to play a sport as a living.

rally   In tennis and volleyball, an exchange of shots between the two opposing players or teams.

serve   The action which starts a point in volleyball, tennis and table tennis, when one player hits the ball into play.

stamina   The energy an athlete needs to perform hard physical exercise for long periods of time.

substitutes   Players who don't start a match but come on to replace a teammate during a game.

tiebreaker   A game in tennis used when the score in a set is tied 6-6. A player must be two points ahead of an opponent to win the set.

wild card   An opportunity for a player to take part in a competition or tournament even though they have not qualified in the usual way.

World Cup   The leading football competition for national football teams. World Cup tournaments are held for both men's and women's football.

Books

Outstanding Olympics Clive Gifford (Oxford University Press, 2008)
Volleyball: Know The Game The English Volleyball Association, (A&CBlack, 2006)
How to Improve at Basketball Jim Drewett (Tick Tock, 2008)
Tennis: Training To Succeed Edward Way (Franklin Watts, 2009)
Hockey: Training To Succeed Rita Storey (Franklin Watts, 2009)

Websites

http://www.olympic.org/en/content/Sports/
This webpage lists all the sports in the Olympics. Click on a sport to go to information on how it is played, Olympic champions and much more.

http://www.fifa.com/
FIFA runs world football, including the World Cup. Its website is enormous and contains videos, photos, interviews and results from football all over the world.

http://www.nba.com/
The official website of the NBA is packed with action videos and photos of top basketball players. It has links to webpages about the WNBA for women and basketball all over the world.

http://www.allabouttabletennis.com/index.html
This website tells you about table tennis, its best players and the leading tournaments.

http://www.itftennis.com/
A great starting point to learn about top tennis players and tournaments, with sections on the Olympics and the men's and women's professional circuits.

http://www.fivb.org/
The official website of the organization that runs volleyball around the world. It has playing guides and rules to both volleyball and beach volleyball.

Index